MARMS
in the
MARMALADE

MARMS
in the
MARMALADE

by Diana Morley
pictures by Kathy Rogers

Carolrhoda Books   Minneapolis, Minnesota

Library of Congress Cataloging in Publication Data

Morley, Diana.
    Marms in the marmalade.

    (A Carolrhoda on my own book)
    Summary: A whimsical look, in verse, at the way words
are put together, e.g., "Since PANcakes are always made
in a PAN, are PANdas and PANthers too?"
    1. English language—Word formation—Juvenile
literature. [1. English language—Wit and humor]
I. Rogers, Kathy, ill. II. Title. III. Series.
PE1175.M62   1984 428.1'0207   83-23982
ISBN 0-87614-258-7 (lib. bdg.)

    2 3 4 5 6 7 8 9 10 92 91 90 89 88 87 86 85

for Jennifer, whose discovery of marms in her marmalade sandwich started the whole thing

Words are usually made in a logical way,
or so I've always thought,
but on looking more closely I would say
they are silly as often as not.

SALTy means having a lot of SALT.

DEWy means covered with DEW.

So, SKINny means covered with lots of SKIN?

I don't think so. Do you?

I've seen many ANTs in an ANThill,
but in the ANTarctic? I doubt it.

Imagine the CAT in CATerpillar.
An insect that purrs? Think about it.

I've made ROLLerskates ROLL
and SNAPdragons SNAP.
Do you think I could ask
a NAPkin to NAP?

MOONlight shines from the MOON, all right,
and SUNlight from the SUN,
but HEADlight from a HEAD? The sight
would make a giant run!

Since PANcakes are always made in a PAN,
are PANdas and PANthers too?

Do CANaries circle 'round garbage CANs
like bats around witches' brew?

I've noticed the WATER in WATERmelon.

On GRAPEs from a GRAPEvine I've fed.

But those can't be MARMs in the MARMalade

piled high in a heap on my bread!

If POPcorn POPs,
are HAZElnuts HAZEy?
Do TURNips TURN,
or are they too lazy?

Is a DENTist covered
with DENTs?

Does a CARpenter
look like a CAR?

Do you think that PENguins
can write with a PEN?

DEAR MOM,
The weather
has been just
GREAT. COLD
AND ICY.

Would a BARber
trim hair on a BAR?

Can a kingFISHer FISH with a POLEcat's POLE?

Can sailors strum golden HARPoons?

The wings of a HUMmingbird do seem to HUM,
but I can't remember the tunes.

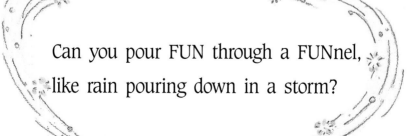

Can you pour FUN through a FUNnel,
like rain pouring down in a storm?

And how about FUR on a FURnace—
is that what keeps it so warm?

Whenever you take a BATH in the BATHtub,
remember how sensible most words are.

But also remember, MARMS
taught in a schoolhouse,

most certainly *not* in a MARMalade jar!